IF YOU CAN'T BE CORRECTED,
YOU CAN'T BE COVERED

by Norman H. Lyons, Jr.

IF YOU CAN'T BE CORRECTED,
YOU CAN'T BE COVERED

by Norman H. Lyons, Jr.

NVP

NUVISION PUBLISHING

Books may be ordered through booksellers
or by contacting:
Norman H. Lyons, Jr.
PO Box 86
Uniondale NY 11553

ISBN# 978-1-5136-8223-5

NUVISION PUBLISHING

PO Box 4455 | Wilmington NC
www.nuvisiondesigns.biz

Printed in the United States of America.

Table of Contents

I Timothy 4:1-3

(1) I charge thee therefore before God and The Lord Jesus Christ, who shall judge the quick and the dead at his appearing and his kingdom;

(2) Preach the word; be instant in season, out of season; reprove, rebuke, exhort with all long suffering and doctrine.

(3) For the time will come when they will not endure sound doctrine; but after their own lusts shall they heap to themselves teachers, having itching ears;

Chapter 1

IF YOU CAN'T BE CORRECTED, YOU CAN'T BE COVERED

Scenario 1

There was a news report regarding a

young lady who did not abide by her parent's curfew. She came home late and there was a dispute. She claims her parents kicked her out, but her parents claimed she left home on her own. She is reportedly now living with the family of the lawyer who is helping her sue her parents for college tuition.

Scenario 2

There was a young woman who became pregnant while living at home with her parents. When asked how he was coping with the situation the father said, "My daughter walked out from underneath my covering and this is what happened. She wouldn't listen to me and now we are here.

Scenario 3

There was a young man who was warned by his mother to stay out of a certain house in the neighborhood. He didn't follow her instructions and he kept going to that house. It was there he had his first sexual experience and impregnated a young woman. When the parents of the couple met, both parents stated that their child knew better.

Scenario 4

There was a young preacher who became fascinated with an older preacher's preaching technique. So, he started going to the older preacher's office on a regular basis. The young man was warned to stay out of that preacher's office, but he didn't listen and take heed. The older preacher introduced the younger preacher to alcohol and the younger preacher subsequently became an alcoholic.

In the ***first case scenario,*** the girl disobeyed her curfew and is now suing her parents for financial support. She wants her parent's money, but she didn't respect her parent's standards.

In the **second scenario,** the daughter rejected the authority and influence of her father. Therefore, she became easy pickings for the dude on the street that wanted to take advantage of her.

In the **third scenario,** the young man did the opposite of what his mother told him not to do. As a result, he prematurely became an expectant father.

In the **fourth scenario,** the young preacher submitted to the one Satan sent to corrupt him instead of submitting to the one God sent to correct him.

These are just a few examples of the sad reality that *if you can't be corrected, you can't be covered.* It is not easy to properly administer correction or be corrected today. It is annoying and unpleasant. It is tedious, tiring, and time consuming. It requires a lot of love and exactitude. It's embarrassing, humiliating and many times it is unappreciated.

Sometimes, depending on the class of people who are involved, it can even become violent.

The devil has deceived the culture, and many in the church, that nobody's ever wrong anymore. The devil will tell you "it's not wrong, it's just an alternate lifestyle." He will tell you, "it's not wrong, it's an orientation." But the worse thing the devil can tell you is that "Its God." That's how church folk roll. When some of them try to justify themselves when faced with correction, they cry, "The Lord told me," "the Spirit led me," "God revealed to me." Sometimes, I want to ask some folk, "What warlord, what demon spirit and what false God are you referring to?" The Spirit of the true and living God does not act unseemly.

In the church, correction is described as **rebuke** and **reprove**. In our text, rebuke means, "censure or admonish: forbid and straightly charge. Reprove means to confute, admonish, convict, convince, tell a fault. First, I must explain in a practical sense what these words mean and then I will explain why they are hard to do.

Rebuke means to censure. The American Heritage Dictionary defines censure as "An expression of disapproval, blame, or criticism. An official rebuke, to criticize severely."

Reprove means to confute. The American Heritage Dictionary defines confute as "to prove to be wrong or false: refute decisively."

Practically speaking, reproof is an attempt to convince someone of the truth of their wrongdoing. You have to tell them what they did wrong with a view to correction for improvement and growth.

A rebuke is stronger and carries more weight than a reproof. A rebuke is an official declaration that is designed to express the severity of an inordinate action. It communicates that someone has exceeded the reasonable limits and has become disorderly. It preserves the integrity of an institution, the church or any other entity. It can also prevent the occurrence from being repeated.

Reproving and **rebuking** are extremely difficult to do in the church today because most of the time when a person does something wrong or inordinate, they think they are right. If a person does something out of order and does not truthfully know it was wrong, they are shocked when they are reproved or rebuked for it. They are shocked and usually go into defense mode. They go into defense mode because they are caught off guard and feel like they are being mistreated or attacked. Sometimes you have a worst-case scenario when someone truly knows that a particular act is wrong but they do it any way with the intent to test or entrap a member, a leader or the Pastor.

There was a pastor who walked into the sanctuary and noticed that a preacher had fallen asleep in the pastor's chair. The preacher had assumed a seat and position that was expressly reserved for the pastor. The Pastor discerned that the preacher actually wanted him to rebuke them so they could have an excuse to do what they already intended to do. Because there were no witnesses, the Pastor refrained from reproving or rebuking the young preacher with the understanding, "*Reprove not a scorner lest he hate thee: rebuke a wise man, and he will love thee. Give instruction to a wise man, and he will be yet wiser: teach a just man, and he will increase in learning.*" (Proverbs 9:8, 9)

In other words, like they say in other parts of the country, "you don't kick a skunk." After all, the Pastor said he had sat in the chair long enough to know it was bad for your back anyway. When something like this happens, the Pastor has to discern spiritually or investigate naturally to determine what really happened and what was intended.

Another factor that makes reproving and rebuking difficult is when there is a public occurrence, especially in a formal church service. Someone does something out of order in front of the congregation. Someone does something out of order in a Sunday service, a special service, such as a wedding, funeral, ordination, etc. Even though everybody may have seen and heard the same thing, people interpret what they see in different ways. Then opinions are formed, comments are made, that are good, bad and indifferent.

One common experience is that reproof and rebuke usually expose the cliques in the church. If a member of a clique is corrected, then all the members in the clique galvanize behind their friend. In such instances the problem is multiplied by the amount of people in the clique.

Another unfortunate possibility is how reproof and rebuke can affect an entire family.   It's hard not to take it personal when a blood relative is reproved or rebuked. It's extremely difficult when the correction is done in public.

Unfortunately, there are times when public rebuke is necessary.   If it is not administered publicly, the offense may be repeated by the same person or someone else.   This causes a greater credibility problem that can lead to a chronic strong hold in a church.   Public rebuke sends a clear message that the leader is serious about the issue at hand that needs to be corrected.   Some people don't take the pastor seriously until he or she publicly rebukes them.   Allow me to explain. One

Sunday a pastor stood up in the pulpit and made reference to a long-term problem in the church. It offended some people. There were private discussions about the validity, timing and fidelity of the strong statements. Consequently, there were three categories of people who left the church. The real problem was that the congregation heard the public rebuke from the pulpit, but not the 8-10 years of private reproof. It takes a tremendous toll on the leader when he or she has to repeat themselves for almost a decade with no improvement. But when the reproof has not been regarded or respected for 8-10 years the leader has been toiling in longsuffering. This kind of situation hurts the leader and the church.

Some people would rather leave their local church all together rather than admit and submit to correction. There were two church leaders who were laughing and joking on a Sunday morning while their pastor was preaching. The pastor came down from the pulpit, walked over to them and rebuked them for distracting him in the middle of his message. The two leaders were shocked, embarrassed and angry. The congregation was divided in their opinions as to who was right or who was wrong. One leader made an appointment to speak to the pastor. In the meeting the leader said, "You know pastor, I almost rebuked you for what you did Sunday morning. You know you are not the only one that has a vision, I have a vision for this church too." The pastor said, "You don't cast vision for the church, Pastors do. If you have two visions for the church, you instantly have Di-vision." The leader disagreed and left the church along with the other leader and their families. Interestingly enough, the leader that was corrected did not mention his childish conduct while the pastor was preaching. The pastor's rebuke was not done in a vacuum. Because these two grown men did not correct themselves, they had to be corrected.

One of the reasons why reproof and rebuke are extremely difficult to accept is because the principle is not readily taught or discussed. Much of what we hear by way of popular teaching and preaching is primarily motivational speaking. Motivational speaking from the pulpit produces weak and wayward Christians.

Motivational speaking inspires you, but it doesn't strengthen, settle or establish you.

Listen again to what Paul told Timothy he was charged to do as a Pastor. *"Preach the word; be instant in season, out of season; reprove, rebuke, exhort with all long suffering and doctrine." (KJV) "Preach the message, be ready whether it is convenient or not, reprove, rebuke, exhort with complete patience and instruction." (NET)*

"Proclaim the message; be persistent whether the time is favorable or unfavorable; convince, rebuke, and encourage, with the utmost patience in teaching." (NRSV)

There are four categories of pastoral oratorical responsibilities; reproof, rebuke, encourage and teaching (doctrine or instruction). If a Pastor only encourages the flock without correcting or teaching, he or she will be derelict in their responsibility. Why would a Pastor be derelict in this regard? I submit to you that reproof and rebuke doesn't pay as well as encouragement and sound doctrine. Sadly enough, so many preachers and pastors are greedy for filthy lucre. The profit motive, the money driven minister syndrome has corrupted the ranks of ministry. I preached the message years ago entitled, "Don't Let Your Ministry Become Industry."

Job 5:17

"Behold, happy is the man whom God correcteth: therefore despise not thou the chastening of the Almighty:"

"Therefore blessed is the man whom God corrects, so do not despise the discipline of the Almighty." (NET)

Chapter 2

A POSITIVE END TO A PAINFUL PROCESS

This verse is part of a speech given to Job by Eliphaz. The name Eliphaz means "God is his strength." Eliphaz was the chief and oldest of Job's three friends or comforters. It's interesting to note that the name Job means "persecuted." One day

27

God's strength sits down to talk to God's persecuted. Our verse is actually the conclusion to Eliphaz's counsel to Job. It is here we find a marvelous insight into the positive and progressive aspect of correction. Eliphaz teaches us that there is a positive end to a painful process.

There is a billboard about exercise that says, "Pain is the feeling of weakness leaving your body." We all would probably exercise more if it were painless. Likewise, we would be more receptive to correction if it were painless. We would be more open to it if it were not so embarrassing. We would be more appreciative of it if it were not so humiliating. Yet, this is the process that

God has chosen to prepare us for the best he has to offer us. God's best often comes through a painful process.

The word "correcteth" in the verse means to argue, to chasten, convince, dispute, judge, maintain, plead, reason, rebuke and reproof. This is the painful process. The word "happy" in our verse means blessed, happiness due to being straight, on the level, right and honest. (Strongs) You will note the NET translation renders the word "happy" as blessed. Listen to the explanation in their annotations, The word "blessed" is often rendered "happy." But happy relates to what happens. "Blessed" is a reference to the heavenly bliss of the one who is right with God. This is the positive end to the painful process.

Our generation glorifies the positive, to the extent that if anything involves negativity, we run away from it. But there would be no positive if there were no negative. Most of the athletes will tell you, their teams often hated the pains of practice but loved the thrill of victory in the games. Most bakers don't love the heat of the oven but enjoy the sweetness of the cake. Most grooms don't really like all the particulars of the wedding traditions, ceremonies and etc. but they love the honeymoon. Most mothers don't like the labor pains of birth but love the blessing of the baby.

Negative and positive have always co-existed. Therefore, we must learn how to analyze, get past ourselves, and adjust. When we think we are above correction, we become prime candidates for correction. When we think this word of reproof, rebuke and correction could never be for me, we have not gotten past ourselves. You don't ever want to be the greatest thing that never was. So patiently and humbly submit to the correction of the Lord so your life can bear the blessing of The Lord.

The verse goes on to say, *"despise not thou the chastening of the Almighty." (KJV)* and *"do not despise the discipline of the Almighty." (NET).* The word "despise" in the verse means to spurn, to disappear, abhor, cast away, disdain, reject, and become a vile person. [Spurn- to reject or refuse disdainfully.] We are admonished not to despise the chastening or discipline of the Almighty. Sadly, in so many cases we do just that. Many people spurn the pastor who rebukes them. Many people disappear from the church that they were chastised in. Many people reject the bad news about themselves, not realizing the good news is somebody loves you enough to tell you the truth. Many people even become vile and vicious in reaction to correction. When a person becomes *that toxic, listen to what usually happens: "Thine own wickedness shall correct thee, and thy backslidings, shall reprove thee: know therefore and see that it is an evil thing and bitter, that thou hast forsaken The Lord thy God, and that my fear is not in thee, saith The Lord God of hosts." (Jeremiah 2:19)*

Now that we have taken Job 5:17 apart, allow me to put it back together again.

"Behold, happy is the man whom God correcteth: therefore despise not thou the chastening of the Almighty." Behold what?

33

What are we to see? Behold! What are we to take note of that confirms the argument of Eliphaz? In order to see the happy and blessed state of the one God corrects, you must note the closing arguments of Eliphaz. His closing argument is found in verses 18-27.

Sometimes we have to let the Bible speak for itself.

18- For he maketh sore, and bindeth up: he woundeth, and his hands make whole.

19- He shall deliver thee in six troubles: yea, in seven there shall no evil touch thee.

20- In famine he shall redeem thee from death: and in war from the power of the sword.

21- Thou shalt be hid from the scourge of the tongue: neither shalt thou be afraid of destruction when it cometh.

22- At destruction and famine thou shalt laugh: neither shalt thou be afraid of the beasts of the earth.

23- For thou shalt be in league with the stones of the field: and the beasts of the earth.

24-And thou shalt know thy tabernacle shall be in peace; and thou shalt visit thy habitation, and shalt not sin.

25-Thou shalt know also that thy seed shall be great, and thine offspring as the grass of the earth.

26- Thou shalt come to thy grave in a full age, like as a shock of corn cometh in his season.

27-Lo this, we have searched it, so it is; hear it, and know thou it for thy good.

I rest my case
on the Word of God.

Chapter 3

REBUKE AND RESTORATION

When I was a little boy there was a minister in our church who was rebuked and silenced. Back then when you were silenced, you had to continue to come to church. The preacher was not allowed to sit in the pulpit. He had to sit in the pew with the other saints. He could not preach or lead out in the service like he did before he was silenced. He was being disciplined for something that he had done wrong.

One Sunday night during his silencing he was allowed to sing in the devotional service. He sang and then the anointing fell on him and he really sang until the entire church was lifted high into the presence of God. People were praising God: some were crying, others were worshipping, and the presence of God lingered a long time. After a while the pastor stood up and asked the minister to come back to the pulpit. The pastor restored the minister that night and the disciplinary action of silencing was ended.

The reason why the discipline of rebuke and restoration worked back then and rarely works now can be embodied in one word. That word is, **"RESPECT."** Back then we had it, today we don't. Back then the leaders and the people had respect for God and God's house. There was a standard and the standard was high. The standard was respected. When people were disorderly or inordinate, they were disciplined and corrected. The leaders had to apply it and the people had to adhere to rebuke and restoration. That's why we had more power in the church than we have now. Although rebuke was not pleasant, it preserved the integrity of the church. Rebuke helped to maintain order in the house of God.

Currently, we are suffering because in so many churches there is no restraint. Without restraint you can't be a good disciple. The church must return to the place where we can produce good disciples of the Lord Jesus Christ.

Chapter 4

A SLAP IN THE FACE

Back in the day there was an old school Pastor that had a peculiar way of rebuking some of the saints. Although I don't advocate doing what he did, it was effective when he did it. From time to time the Pastor would call a member up to the podium and gently slap them on the cheek. He would tap your cheek and stare you straight in the eye for a moment and then tell you to sit down.

One Sunday he called a teenage young man to come to him and he slapped him on the cheek and stared at him and then told him to sit down. When the other young people tried to make the young man feel abused by the leader, he said, "I rather he slap me then tell what I did that caused him to slap me." The young man understood exactly why the Pastor slapped him. He endured the rebuke and eventually became a church leader that built a great work for the Lord. He credits the leadership and influence of his "face slapping" pastor for his good success. The slap was crude and totally unacceptable for today, but the young man appreciated it and it worked.

Chapter 5

THE WOMAN WITH THE RED DRESS

There was a woman who had a bad habit of wearing revealing clothes to church. Sometimes the dresses were too short. Sometimes the dresses were too tight. Sometimes the dresses were see-through.

After a while, the pastor had enough and after one bad wardrobe Sunday he confronted the woman. When he asked the woman to refrain from wearing revealing clothing to church, she responded by saying, "My husband likes it when I dress like that." The pastor simply told her, "But this is not your husband's house. This is God's house, and I am the pastor and I'm asking you not to come to church looking like that." The woman's husband was a church leader who supported well. He became offended by the pastor's reproof of his wife's attire. So, he and the family left the church except for his son. The son stayed. Although the pastor had to endure the wrath of the woman and her husband, he maintained the integrity of the church. He stood for a standard. Surprisingly enough, the other women in the church agreed with the leader. They were tired of the woman parading her body around their husbands and sons in the church. If the

Pastor had not taken a stand against the inordinate dress of the woman, he and the church would have lost credibility. They left but the church didn't lose.

Chapter 6

I WANT YOU TO WORK ON THAT

There was a young preacher who gave a sermon in his home church. After the service, a church mother asked to speak to him on the side. She complemented him and said that she saw a great future for him. In addition to her compliments, she quickly pointed out some errors that she wanted him to correct. She said, "I want you to work on that." The young preacher accepted her compliment as well as her correction.

This woman was not just an ordinary

church mother. She was an extraordinary elocutionist. She excelled at writing poems and crafting tributes to honor people in appreciation and anniversary services. The young preacher would sit and be spellbound by her precision and oratorical presence. She had a profound impact upon him. This made it easier for him to receive correction from her. He went on to work on his weaknesses and even adopted the mother's approach and technique.

One day, as a much older preacher, someone complimented him on his ability to have remarks and give tributes. He quickly attributed his effectiveness to the example and influence of the church mother who corrected him. He said many people may never know her name or her tremendous gift, but he acknowledged her phenomenal gift and impact upon his writing and speaking. He further explained that there were times while he was composing, he would ask himself, "how would Mother approach this piece?" Recalling her compositions, approach, and execution helped him to perfect his craft and bless many people. The preacher realized the value of the mother's correction. He respected her and benefited from her tutelage. Her correction created a hunger within him to grow and achieve mastery. Her correction didn't kill the young man but rather it stimulated him.

She wasn't a butcher but a surgeon. The sting of her correction only lasted a minute, but the blessing of her correction has lasted a lifetime.

One of the greatest honors this preacher received was when the church mother's daughter asked him to have remarks at her mother's homegoing. He approached the assignment with the same intensity and exactitude her example taught him. Of course, he was misunderstood for it, but it blessed her grieving daughter.

Chapter 7

YES SIR BISHOP

There was an elder in a local church who had repeatedly overstepped their boundaries of authority. Eventually, the pastor had to address the situation. When the pastor spoke to the elder about the problem, at first the elder was defensive. But in the middle of the discussion the elder looked at the pastor and simply said, "Yes sir Bishop." When the elder said, "Yes sir Bishop" the conversation took a positive turn. They were able to resolve the situation and the elder grew to become one of the strongest leaders in the church.

I submit to you that something very revelatory happened on the inside of the elder. The elder realized that the proper response to rebuke was submission. Unlike so many others who choose to be argumentative, this elder humbled himself and understood the overall impact of his conduct on the continuity of ministry. The elder grew and was given more responsibility because he proved that he could be trusted.

If you CANNOT endure rebuke
you CANNOT be trusted.
If you CAN endure rebuke
you CAN be trusted.

In this scenario, rebuke did not break the elder it made the elder.

Chapter 8

I AM NOT GOING TO TAKE THIS

There was an elder who was asked by his pastor to take the lead in a segment of the Pastor's Anniversary. In essence, he was being asked to raise a certain amount of money which he gladly did. After the Anniversary, the pastor called him into a meeting with the Pastors Aide Committee. It was then that the Pastors Aide President accused the elder of usurping authority over her. As the elder waited for the pastor to explain that He asked the elder to do what he did, the pastor surprisingly said, "Some people just have bad blood."

Needless to say, the elder was shocked and felt betrayed by his pastor. In wisdom, the elder apologized and the meeting was closed.

As the elder was driving home from the meeting, he began to boil in outrage over what had just happened to him. He abruptly made a U-turn in the middle of the street and sped back to the office. He fully intended to express his outrage to the pastor but when the door to the office opened, he saw another pastor sitting there whom he highly respected. He slowly stepped back out of the office telling his pastor never mind. This is a classic example of abuse of power. The elder was a victim of manipulation. Thank God there was a divine roadblock to his anger and retaliation. The elder was not only rebuked but insulted and cursed inappropriately. The depth of the injury can be measured by the fact that the elder's father was a well-known backslidden preacher. The pastor's statement opened up a wound in the elder that was deep and sore. The elder clearly understood he had to leave that church in order to be healed again and continue his ministry. Ultimately, he forgave the pastor and was able to pray for him in his hour of need many years later.

The takeaway is that sometimes the responsibility of rebuke can be grossly abused. Yet the response to this travesty has to be forgiveness and reconciliation. Nothing less will do. It is difficult but doable, nevertheless. The elder would have destroyed his reputation and future in his denomination if he had given in to his rage. Ultimately, God judged that pastor and the other culprits in this scenario. The pastor eventually disgraced himself and had to leave town. The elder's reputation was preserved, and he went on to ascend to the higher echelon of the church.

The lesson learned from this account is this: when rebuke is abused, and misapplied, God will judge and vindicate the innocent. It may take some time but God can be trusted. If you are rebuked incorrectly, remember to trust God and not your own sense of self justification. God's grace will abound greatly towards you and you will grow, prosper and flourish. As crude as it may sound, the old saints were right,

"If you can take it, you can make it."

Chapter 9

THE BREAKING AND THE BLESSING

Long before I was a pastor and bishop, my pastor died, and the Jurisdictional Bishop assumed the leadership of our local church. At the time, I was just a licensed minister. In this transitional period, we were struggling to grasp a sense of normalcy. So, the church decided to have a special service to honor our senior citizens. Oddly enough, they asked me *(the youngest preacher in the church)* to preach for that service. In the middle of the message, the bishop walks through the door. He walks up to the pulpit and sits behind me while I finished my little message. When I was finished, he stood up and publicly rebuked me for about 20-30 minutes saying, "preaching like that you will never be ordained in this church." When he was finished the people started shouting and dancing. While the people were rejoicing over my humiliation, I temporarily went blind. I could hear them, but I could not see. My sight shut down and I was still. Although I didn't quite understand his explanation for why he rebuked me, he was the bishop, and I was trained to submit to his authority.

After my sight returned, I walked to where the bishop was seated and kneeled before him and said these words, "Bishop please pray for me because I want to get it right." For the first time in my life, I saw fear in the bishop's face. I didn't understand why and before I could think another thought, an older visiting pastor reached over the bishop and put his hand in front of my face and said, "Young man, don't say another word, you just passed your test." I looked at the bishop then I looked at the visiting pastor and got up off my knees and returned to my seat. When the Bishop stood up to give the benediction, he said I want to see the trustees and the young man in the office after the service. I dreaded having to go into the office not knowing what in the world to expect but I did it, nevertheless. At the conclusion of the trustee board meeting, the Bishop dismissed everybody except for me. When we were alone, he said, "If it's the last thing I do, I'm going to ordain you because you have the right spirit." Now I'm really confused.

We leave the office and I walk home to the projects where I lived and sat on the bench all night until the next day. My mother watched me from the window as the saints called her all night to check on me and to offer their opinions as to whether the bishop was right or wrong. For me the question was, what should I do? Did I have what it takes to endure rebuke, correction and humiliation? All night, I thought about all my options and the possible outcomes. As the sun was rising and the darkness was giving way to light, I remembered the advice an older minister gave me immediately after the service before I went into the office. He said, "purchase a good study bible and a good dictionary and study." And that is exactly what I did.

After this incident the Bishop took a personal interest in me and told me he was training me. He allowed me to go to Haiti on a missionary assignment. He sent me to assist a pastor who was fighting cancer. He ordained me, married me, and covered me like a son.

People have often asked me whether I thought the bishop was right or wrong to rebuke me the way he did. I developed what I thought was a good response. I would say, "It doesn't matter whether he was right or wrong, all that mattered was how I responded." The public only heard what he said from the pulpit. I was the only one that heard what he said to me in the office. The record will reflect that the bishop kept his word and did what he said. He ordained me in the same church and in front of the same people he told I would never be ordained preaching like I did.

The lesson that I learned from that

experience was that if you could take the bishop's beating you were qualified for the bishop's blessing. The blessing was far greater than the beating, so it was worth it. Once I learned the leadership style of the bishop, I was able to adjust and adapt. I went on to have a tremendous relationship with the bishop. By the way, in the reformation I grew up in at that time, *"The Bishop is always right."*

Regardless of the pain and embarrassment, open rebuke did not destroy me. It helped to make me. Rebuke tested my solidarity to God, church authority, and my calling. It proved to be one of the best things that could have happened to me at that time.

The other benefit of that painful experience was that it knocked a lot of pride out of me. It humbled me flat on my face in front of the whole church. I was broken into pieces, but the operation was a success. The bishop pounded a lot of pride out of me and for this I am grateful. From that point on I did everything he told me to do, exactly the way he told me to do it. To his credit, he never told me to do anything inordinate or questionable. He covered, cultivated, and elevated me in ministry. He used rebuke to make a man and minister out of me.

CONCLUSION

Correction is like a surgery. Although the process is not pleasant, it produces the restoration of health.

Hebrews 12: 10-11 (10) "For they verily for a few days chastened us after their own pleasure; but he for our profit, that we might be partakers of his holiness.

(11) Now no chastening for the present seemeth to be joyous, but grievous: nevertheless afterward it yieldeth the peaceable fruit of righteousness unto them are exercised thereby."

The church benefits from the ministry of rebuke and correction. However, it must be done in an appropriate manner in the spirit of love. The purpose of rebuke is for the elimination of error. If the leader and the laity honor the legitimacy of the ministry of rebuke, the church will be pure and powerful. Only the enemy would delegitimize the efficacy of rebuke so he could weaken the church. If our parents never corrected us, we would be wayward and lawless. The end result of waywardness and lawlessness is destruction.

In order to keep the church upright and potent, we must reinstitute rebuke to maintain the integrity of the church.

I remember participating in a consecration of a bishop. We had to purchase special garments. I became annoyed at a strip of material on one of my garments and I said, "Maybe I should just cut this little piece off." A fellow pastor quickly said to me, "If you cut that piece off, you will compromise the integrity of the garment." He was absolutely right, and I endured the annoyance of the strip of fabric and wore the garment according to its design.

Likewise, the church has to continue the correction of rebuke in order to preserve the integrity of the church. You cannot have a viable church if there is no mechanism of rebuke and correction for inordinate conduct. In order for us to be strong, we must be circumspect. There must be order in the church. Order must be upheld in the church so that the sheepfold does not become a zoo. We are safer when pastors love the flock of God enough to correct wayward activity. A lack of correction is a lack of love. God bless the pastor who will lovingly apply correction in order to build character into the congregation. God bless the people who will endure correction and rebuke in order to be built up in God.

Correction is rarely initially kind but ultimately kind.

Blessed are the people who know that it is better to be corrected and covered than to be appeased and uncovered. An uncovered church is vulnerable to error and heresy. An uncovered church is like a lawn littered with weeds. An uncovered church is in danger of being devoured by the lions and the bears. A real shepherd will correct the flock of God and cover them. A real flock will understand **THAT IF WE CAN'T BE CORRECTED, WE CAN'T BE COVERED.**

Reference Scriptures on
Rebuke, Reproof, and Correction

Jeremiah 2:19
"Your own wickedness will correct you,
And your apostasies will reprove you."
(NAS)

Jeremiah 2: 30
"In vain I have struck your sons; They
accepted no chastening. Your sword
has devoured your prophets like a
destroying lion."

Deuteronomy 28:20
"The Lord shall send upon thee cursing,
vexation and rebuke, in all that thou settest
thine hand unto for to do, until thou be
destroyed, and until thou perish quickly;
because of the wickedness of thy doings,
whereby thou hast forsaken me."

II Kings 19:3
"And they said unto him, Thus saith Hezekiah, This is a day of trouble, and of rebuke, and blasphemy: for the children are come to the birth, and there is not strength to bring forth."

Psalm 80:16
"It is burned with fire it is cut down: they perish at the rebuke of thy countenance."

Proverbs 27: 5
"Open rebuke is better than secret love."

Ecclesiates 7:5
"It is better to hear the rebuke of the wise, than for a man to hear the song of fools."

Isaiah 30:17
"One thousand shall flee at the rebuke of one; at the rebuke of five shall ye flee: till ye be left as a beacon upon the top of a mountain, and as an ensign on an hill."

Isaiah 50:2
"Wherefore, when I came, was there no man? When I called, was there none to answer? Is my hand, shortened at all, that it cannot redeem? Or have I no power to deliver? Behold at my rebuke I dry up the sea, I make the rivers a wilderness: their fish stinketh because there is no water, and dieth for thirst.

Philippians 2:15
"That ye may be blameless and harmless, the sons of God, without rebuke in the midst of a crooked and perverse nation, among whom ye shine as lights in the world;"

Psalm 6:1
"O Lord, rebuke me not in thine anger, neither chasten me in thy hot displeasure."

Proverbs 9:7-9

"He that reproveth a scorner getteth to himself shame: and he that rebuketh a wicked man getteth himself a blot."
(8) Reprove not a scorner lest he hate thee: rebuke a wise man, and he will love thee.
(9) Give instruction to wise a man, and he will be yet wiser: teach a just man, and he will increase in learning."

Proverbs 28:23

"He that rebuketh a man afterwards, shall find more favour than he that flattereth with the tongue."

Isaiah 2:4

"And he shall judge among the nations, and shall rebuke many people: and they shall beat their swords into plowshares, and their spears into pruning hooks: nation shall not lift up sword against nation, neither shall they learn war any more."

Zechariah 3:2
"And the Lord said unto Satan, The Lord rebuke thee, O Satan; even the Lord that hath chosen Jerusalem rebuke thee: is not this a brand plucked out of the fire?

Jude 9
"Yet Michael the archangel, when contending with the devil he disputed about the body of Moses, durst not, bring against him a railing accusation, but said, The Lord rebuke thee."

Proverbs 12:1
"Whoever loves discipline loves knowledge, But he who hates reproof is stupid." (NAS)

Luke 17:3
"Be on your guard! If your brother sins, rebuke him; and if he repents, forgive him." (NAS)

I Timothy 5:20
"Those who continue in sin, rebuke in the presence of all, so that the rest also may be fearful of sinning."(NAS)

II Timothy 4:2
"preach the word: be ready in season and out of season; reprove, rebuke, exhort, with great patience and instruction." (NAS)

Titus 1:13
"This testimony is true. For this cause reprove them severely that they may be sound in the faith." (NAS)

Titus 2:15
"These things speak and exhort and reprove with all authority. Let no one disregard you." (NAS)

Hebrews 12: 5-6
"and you have forgotten the exhortation which is addressed to you as sons,

"May son, do not regard lightly the discipline of the lord, nor faint when you are reproved by him; for those whom the lord loves he disciplines, and he scourges every son whom he receives." (NAS)

Revelation 3:19
"Those whom I love, I reprove and discipline; be zealous therefore, and repent. (NAS)

The ABC's of Salvation

1. Admit that you have sinned. "For all have sinned, and come short of the glory of God." (Romans 3:23)

2. Believe on Jesus Christ the Savior. "For God so loved the world, that he gave his only begotten Son, that whosoever Believeth in Him should not perish, but have everlasting life." (John 3:16)

3. Confess. "That if thou shalt confess with thy mouth the Lord Jesus and shalt believe in thine heart that God hath raised him from the dead, thou shalt be saved, For with the heart man believeth unto righteousness; and with the mouth confession is made unto salvation." (Romans 10: 9-10)

A Prayer for Salvation

"Heavenly Father in Jesus name, I confess that I am a sinner. Forgive me for my sin and save me. I repent of my sin. I believe in my heart on the Lord Jesus Christ and confess with my mouth that I accept Him as my personal Lord and Saviour. Thank you for saving me. Amen."

BIOGRAPHICAL SKETCH OF THE AUTHOR

Bishop Norman Lyons, Jr. is the founder and senior pastor of the Fountain of Life Church in Uniondale, New York. In addition to his national ministry, he has also done missionary work in Haiti, Nigeria, West Africa and Italy. Bishop Lyons has served as an executive council member of the International Council of Local Churches. He has also served as a member of M.E.C.C.A. For seven years Bishop Lyons was a Board Member of the New York Call hosted by Pastor Donnie McClurkin. Bishop Lyons is Chaplain Emeritus for the Long Island Conference of Clergy.

At the time of this writing, Bishop Lyons has been preaching for 42 years. He has been married to his darling wife, Pastor Sharon, for 41 years. They have pastored the Fountain of Life Church for 38 years.

Norman and Sharon are the grateful parents of two daughters, Juliet and Jasmine. They also have been blessed with a son-in-love, Joaquin, Juliet's husband.